ASSERTIVENESS

ASSERTIVENESS

A POSITIVE PROCESS

*Dr. Barrie Hopson
and Mike Scally*

Pfeiffer
& COMPANY

Amsterdam • Johannesburg • London
San Diego • Sydney • Toronto

Published in association with

Publisher: Pfeiffer/Mercury Books

Published in the UK by Mercury Books: This edition published by:
Pfeiffer & Company
8517 Production Avenue
San Diego, CA 92121-2280 USA

This publication is designed to provide accurate and authoritative information in regard to the subject matter covered. It is sold with the understanding that the publisher is not engaged in rendering legal, accounting, or other professional service. If legal advice or other expert assistance is required, the services of a competent professional person should be sought. *From a Declaration of Principles jointly adopted by a Committee of the American Bar Association and a Committee of Publishers.*

Editor: JoAnn Padgett
Page Compositor: Susan Odelson
Cover Design: John Odam Design Associates

Library of Congress Cataloging-in-Publication Data
　　Assertiveness: a positive process / Barrie Hopson, and Mike Scally.
　　　　p.　　cm.
　　1. Assertiveness training.　　I. Hopson, Barrie.　　II. Scally, Mike.
III. Title.
RC489.A77B44　　1993
158'.2–dc20　　　　　　　　　　　　　　　　　　　92-50989
　　　　　　　　　　　　　　　　　　　　　　　　　　　　CIP

Printed in the United States of America.

Printing 1 2 3 4 5 6 7 8 9 10

Contents

Preface

Welcome to our series of open learning workbooks! In this brief foreword, we invite you to consider some of our beliefs.

- **We do not need teachers to learn.** Not all of what we know in life was learned through formal education. We can, and do, learn in a whole range of ways, and we learn best when we know our own needs.

- **The best way to help people is to encourage them to help themselves.** Self-help and self-management avoid the dependency which blocks development and burdens ourselves and others.

- **Awareness, knowledge, and skills give us more options in life.** Lack of any of these is a disadvantage; possession of them allows us to live fuller lives, shaping events rather than simply reacting to them.

- **The more able and accomplished we become, the more we fill society's reservoir of talent and contribute to the common good.**

- **It has been said that the future is not what it used to be!** In this, age, the goalposts keep being moved, so increasingly our security needs to come from having information and skills.

The term "lifeskill" came from work based on these beliefs which we began at Leeds University in the 1970s. Our philosophy has been widely applied in education, in industry and commerce, and in the community, inviting people to take charge of their lives and make them satisfying and rewarding.

Until now, Lifeskills have been only available through training courses and teaching programs. With the publication of this series they are now available in a self-help format consistent with the Lifeskills approach because you are in charge of your own learning. Learn at your own pace, in your own time, and apply your learning to your situation. We wish you both enjoyment and success!

Barrie Hopson
Mike Scally

Introduction

Many of us feel, at one time or another, that we lack control in our lives. We may feel confident that we have made the right decisions in life, but still we wonder how it is that others seem always to get what they want, while our wants and needs are overlooked. We might know that we are very good at our job, for example, and feel frustrated when others are picked for special tasks or promotion and our ideas are ignored. Or we may find it difficult to deal with our parents or a partner, and worry about their criticism and the impression we make. These are typical of situations that assertiveness can help us to deal with—and feel better about.

Before we go any further, what do you think assertiveness means?

_____

_____

_____

In this book, we answer the questions "What is assertiveness?" and "How do I become an assertive person?" We begin, in Chapter 1, by describing three types of behavior—assertive, aggressive, and unassertive. We suggest that many of us are capable of being any or all three at different times in our lives. But the aim of this book is to help you, the reader, to become an assertive person. Chapters 2-4 describe dimensions of assertiveness and suggest ways of practicing positive behavior, and Chapters 5-6 add further skills—and sharpen them.

Our objectives (we hope you'll have achieved them by the end of the book) are to

- Help you distinguish assertive, aggressive, and passive behavior.
- Outline the skills that support assertive behavior.
- Ensure that you understand the advantages of being assertive and also the dilemmas.

Before You Start...

This workbook has been written for people wanting to know more about personal self-development. It is about reading and doing, so we have chosen to write it as an open learning workbook.

What is open learning? Open learning is a term used to describe a study program that is very flexibly designed so that it adapts to the needs of individual learners. Some open learning programs involve attendance at a study center of some kind, or contact with a tutor or mentor, but even then attendance times are flexible and suit the individual. This workbook is for you to use at home or at work and most of the activities are for you to complete alone. We sometimes suggest that it would be helpful to talk with a friend or colleague—self-development is easier if there is another person with whom to talk over ideas. But this isn't essential by any means.

With this workbook you can

- Organize your study to suit your own needs.
- Study the material alone or with other people.
- Work through the book at your own pace.
- Start and finish just where and when you want to, although we have indicated some suggested stopping points with a ☕ symbol.

The sections marked Personal Project involve you in more than working through the text. They require you to take additional time—sometimes an evening, sometimes a week. For this reason, we are not giving clear guidelines on how long it will take you to complete this workbook, but the written part of the book will probably take you about six hours to complete.

1

What Is
Assertive
Behavior?

When we are assertive, we tell people what we want, need, or would prefer. We state our preference clearly and confidently, without belittling ourselves or others, without being threatening or putting other people down. Assertive people can initiate conversation; they can compliment others and receive compliments gracefully; they can cope with justified criticism—and they can give it, too. It's a positive way of behaving, that doesn't involve violating the rights of other people. Above all, assertive behavior is appropriate behavior. This can mean that it's appropriate on occasions to be angry, or it can mean choosing not to be assertive in a particular situation or with a particular person.

Body Language

The way we act physically tells people a lot about us. Our body language often reveals how we feel and may show uncertainty, or contradict what we say. A good example is the person who says "I'm not angry," but the clenched teeth, rigid posture, and grim expression reveal angry feelings. Or what about the person who says "I really mean it" but refuses to look you in the eye? In cases like these, the body language contradicts the spoken words.

Can you think of another example?

_____

_____

Which do you think you are more likely to believe, the body language or the spoken words? Why?

_____

_____

_____

The fact is, although we are not always conscious of body language, we instinctively respond to body language rather than to spoken words.

Similarly, gestures such as fiddling with your hair or biting your nails, or not looking at the other person, or hesitant, mumbled, or indistinct speech can all undermine your efforts to assert yourself. How can we be sure that our body language does not contradict, or undermine what we are trying to say?

The answer is to observe yourself in everyday situations. When you find yourself using unhelpful body language, think how you could sit, stand, and use your hands and facial expression to reinforce what you say. Practice speaking clearly and evenly: Don't be ashamed of what you have to say— come right out and own it!

The chart that follows will help you to identify examples of positive or negative body language in different situations. Mark each one with a "+" or "−", depending on whether you think the effect will be good or bad.

Thinking about the ways in which your behavior can affect what you want to say helps you to "unlearn" some bad habits and adopt more positive body language to reinforce your spoken message. You will notice that some examples came up again and again. That's because they are very effective ways of getting your message across clearly, politely, and without causing offense—for example, by smiling.

Checklist of Helpful Body Language

- *Facial expression:* While smiling helps to reinforce that what you say is meant constructively, you should always be genuine—do not smile if you are unhappy, angry, or serious.

Body Language

Situation	Posture	Facial Expression	Hands	Eyes	Tone of Voice
Young person: I've come about the job.	Slouching in chair or standing upright	Smiling or blank expression	Ready for handshake or hands clasped together	Looking directly at person or downcast eyes	Clear, firm or mumbling
Parent: I want you to clean your room—now!	Turning away, busy or facing child	Shaking head or serious	Scratching head or pointing	Glaring or calm, straight look	Vague, unconcerned or emphatic
Employee: I'll finish this tomorrow—I have to go now.	Facing boss or rummaging in drawer	Calm or laughing	Hands visible or hands fiddling	Looking at fingers or direct look	Quick, quiet speech or direct and businesslike
Shopper: I have to go now. I'd like to return these items—they are defective	Head bowed, looking in bag or head upright, facing clerk	Worried frown or smiling	Showing items or stroking hair	Making eye contact or Avoiding eye contact	Clearly spoken or nervous, hesitant
In a line: Excuse me, but I was next.	Standing face to face or approaching from behind	Sad, despairing look or smiling	Hands clenched, raised or hands by side	Looking person in the eye or looking at the floor	Loud, accusing or Calm and clear

Directions: Mark the bottom lefthand corner of each box with a + (good) or − (bad).

- *Eyes and gaze:* The ability to look someone directly in the face and maintain eye contact shows openness and sincerity; looking away will almost always undermine your message.

- *Posture:* Standing still, facing the other person, with your head held high is direct and open; turning away, slouching, or shifting from side to side shows lack of interest or commitment.

- *Hand and arm movements:* Avoid fidgeting, as this distracts attention from your message and from your sincerity. Use your hands to emphasize what you say in a helpful (but not an aggressive) way.

- *Tone of voice:* Whispering, rushing your delivery, or mumbling all suggest that you doubt what you are saying; speak clearly and confidently in an even tone of voice.

- *Own what you say:* "Owning" what you say means making it clear that this is your own opinion, not someone else's, and not what you think someone might like to hear. For example, compare these two conversations between two friends:

A. "Where would you like to go tonight?"
"Wherever you like—I hear that new Italian restaurant is quite good."

B. "Where would you like to go tonight?"
"I'd really like to go to that new restaurant."

In example A, the questioner is no wiser about what the other person feels and has no opportunity to please that person. In example B, the questioner gets a clear answer, knows what the other person would like, and can agree or disagree. Clear statements which begin "I think" or "I would like" are more helpful to the other person.

In some situations, it might be that cooperative words and phrases are more suitable. By cooperative phrases, we mean words that might encourage someone to work or act *with* you rather than *against* you. Think of a situation where you want someone to cooperate with you. What kind of cooperative phrases could you use instead of, "You do this and I'll do that"?

_____

_____

_____

You might have suggested:
"We could . . ."
"Shall we . . . ?"
"Let's try to . . ."

A Few Words on Appropriateness

Assertive behavior is behavior that is suitable, or appropriate, for the occasion. It involves being able to express what is wanted without feeling unduly anxious or hesitant. This is not the same as being "totally honest" about feelings. Neither is it lying. It is a nice balance—being able to express what you feel without offending others or contravening the norms of the situation.

Appropriateness is a social skill that matters a great deal, particularly when learning to be an assertive person. Assertiveness is not a license for bursts of uncontrollable anger because things are not as you think they should be. If there are many "shoulds" and "oughts" in your life, either about yourself or about other people, then you would probably benefit from looking at why you hem yourself in with "I should be . . ." or "I ought to . . . ." You do have the right to be annoyed if someone has violated your rights, but the skill lies in expressing this constructively and, equally importantly, appropriately.

What Is Aggressive Behavior?

What words come to mind when you look at this question? Write all the kinds of aggressive behavior that you can think of in the space that follows.

Do your words for aggressive behavior refer to body language, tone of voice, or other attempts to dominate the situation? Do you like aggressive behavior? Of course not! And certainly no one likes being on the receiving end, whether it's words or actions that are used. Assertive behavior is *not* aggressive behavior.

Aggressive behavior expresses feelings and opinions in a way which punishes, threatens, or puts the other person down. The aim of this behavior is for the person to get his or her own way, no matter what. When we are sarcastic or manipulative, when we spread gossip or make racist or sexist remarks, we are behaving as aggressively as when we physically push someone. If we win, and get what we want, it probably leaves someone else with the bad feeling that he or she has lost. Aside from any ethical considerations, this could set a bad tone for future transactions with that person. Another possible consequence of behaving aggressively is that we might feel guilty later.

Aggressive people often stand too close to others, or they stand when others sit; they point or wag their fingers, and they speak in a loud, scolding tone of voice. They may pat people (on the shoulder, for instance), which patronizes them and reduces the other person's status.

Using your personal experience, note one or two examples of aggressive ways of beginning a conversation.

We thought of
"You must . . ."
"You should . . ."
"You ought . . ."

"You've got to . . ."

"Why haven't you . . .?"

You'll see that, unlike the assertive person, the aggressive person doesn't "own" what he or she says. Rather, an aggressive person immediately transfers the blame to someone else, or directly orders others about without regard for their feelings.

Why Are We Aggressive?

Anyone can become aggressive if threatened or made to feel in the wrong. Aggression is sometimes a sign that there is something wrong with the aggressor, whether he or she simply got out of bed on the wrong side, or something has seriously disrupted his or her life. When you find yourself resorting to aggressive behavior, ask yourself what is wrong and why you are projecting your bad feelings on to someone else. Next time, try to take time out to think of more constructive ways of handling whatever has gone wrong.

What Is Unassertive Behavior?

In what ways are you sometimes unassertive? How do you show it? Think hard, and write down some of the times you have felt unassertive, and the ways you showed it, in the space below.

_____

_____

_____

_____

_____

People with low self-esteem and low self-confidence may feel that they are so unimportant that their own needs aren't valuable and don't deserve attention or care. They tend to leave everything to fate—or to other people. This is passive, or unassertive, behavior.

Unassertive people hope they'll get what they want but expect others to guess their wishes; as a result they often end up feeling angry with others, and think that others should somehow have known what was wanted.

Unassertive body language can include a hesitant stance, with head bowed or held to one side, fidgeting, shifting from one foot to the other, not looking people in the eye, coughing nervously, and looking embarrassed.

Again, from your own experience of yourself or others, can you suggest two ways in which unassertive people might start a sentence?

1. _____

2. _____

You might have said
"I'm sorry . . ."
"Er . . ."
"Um . . ."
"Excuse me . . ."
"Would you mind if . . .?"

Why Are We Unassertive?

By not stating what we really want, we don't give other people a chance to satisfy our needs. Then why don't we just ask outright? What stops us? It might be

- Fear that our request will be turned down—and then what would we do and how would we feel?

- Anxiety about embarrassing someone who does not want to do what would we would like them to do.

- We have been brought up to be "polite," which often means trying to anticipate what someone else really wants by telepathy instead of by asking them! (People cannot read your mind; they can only observe your behavior.)

What Are the Consequences of Being Unassertive?

By not being assertive we often end up feeling angry with ourselves, or annoyed with someone else who somehow should have guessed what we wanted. A person can only take so much. By bottling up feelings for too long, you may suddenly find yourself blowing up at something and acting way out of proportion to the incident itself.

He: "I'm sorry I forgot to mail the letters. I was just too busy."

She: "What do you mean—too busy? You're always too busy. You never think of anyone but yourself. You expect me to run after you—everything revolves around you—you've never got time to pay any attention to me. It's always work, work, work!"

He: "But I only forgot to mail some letters!"

It is useful to note that words like "always" and "never" are rarely true. When someone uses them against you it will almost certainly be an exaggeration. Someone is trying to assert something about you that cannot be true. On the other hand, the very extremity of the words is communicating a message. Listen to the strength of the expression rather than taking the words literally.

What Is So Good About Being Assertive?

The ability to express our feelings constructively and to be open with others about what we want maximizes our chances of getting the personal and professional relationships we want, the job we want, the life we want. Assertive people are more confident, less punishing of others, less frustrated, less anxious. This is well documented in research findings.

Being assertive is another facet of being proactive. By proactive we mean *making* things happen, rather than *letting* them happen. Proactivity is the dimension that is most correlated with high self-esteem and consequently with mental health. All these qualities reinforce each other.

In other words, the more positively we act, the more capable we feel, and this improves our feelings of self-worth. The better we feel about ourselves, the more able we are to act proactively and the less prone we are to self-doubt, anxiety, and depression.

The more assertive we are, the less likely we are to be aggressive, as aggression is usually fueled by frustration. And, of course, people like to be around assertive people because they will be treated fairly and with confidence and respect.

However, there are also disadvantages to assertive behavior. As well as understanding your own behavior and valuing your own feelings, you will come to understand others better and must accept and value their right to express their feelings, too! There are responsibilities as well as rights for the assertive person. (More on this later.) Being an assertive person helps you to communicate your needs, but it doesn't guarantee that you will get more of what you want.

Compromise and negotiation are skills all assertive people have learned. Aggressive people, who are manipulative, use power overtly if they have it and do not concern themselves with the basic rights of others. They are also quite likely to be more successful in terms of power or material wealth. But these people lose out on the emotional support we all need at stressful times in our lives. These people lack the personal wealth that's so significant to us all. However, if you use assertive skills we think you will ultimately be the winner— and certainly you'll sleep easier in your bed at night!

Generally, it seems like a good idea to be an assertive person, so why don't we always, naturally, assert ourselves? Take a few minutes to think about this; let your thoughts go back as far as you can and see if you can suggest two or three reasons why.

_____

_____

_____

You might have suggested

- *Social class.* It is true that there are people with the money, privilege, and educational opportunities to whom assertiveness comes quite naturally. Their background gives them a sense of self-assurance in any situation and this helps them to be assertive. Most of us do not have this self-assurance and are apt to behave less assertively in situations we are not sure of.

- *Gender.* Little girls are taught to defer to the wishes of others; little boys are allowed to assert themselves. This can result in passive behavior in women and aggressive behavior in men. It can also be the other way around. As adults we should try to put aside unproductive passive or aggressive behavior and deal with other people as equals and to "do unto others as we would have them do unto us."

- *Culture or belief system.* Christians, for example, may believe "the meek shall inherit the earth" and that one should "turn the other cheek."

- *Schools.* Teachers often reward the obedient, quiet child. The inquisitive, opinionated child may be seen as disruptive and as a troublemaker.

- *Childhood.* We may have learned early in life that we are praised for doing what others want us to do, or punished for being "strong willed."

A Final Thought

Can you suggest what happens when two assertive people meet?

_____

_____

_____

You might have suggested that they

- Seek alternatives together.
- Compromise.
- Negotiate.

Summary

In this chapter, we have described the main characteristics of assertive, aggressive, and unassertive behavior.

Assertive—stating clearly what we would like to happen, but without a demand that it should.

Aggressive—making sure that we do get what we want, no matter how the other person feels.

Unassertive—doing nothing and hoping, or trying, to get what we want in an indirect way.

We have noted some pluses and minuses of behaving assertively and appropriately, briefly looked at why we are not naturally assertive, and explained what the consequences of unassertive behavior can be.

Take time now to write down two things you have thought or learned about yourself as a result of working through the book so far.

1. _____

_____

2. _____

_____

2

Getting
What
I Want

I n the last chapter, we identified the three main routes people use to get what they want or need. In this chapter, we are inviting you to complete a short quiz. Each situation has three possible answers; we're asking you to decide whether each response is an example of assertive, aggressive, or unassertive behavior. Write down what category of behavior you think each response belongs to—we will provide the answers afterward!

Behavior Quiz

1. You are wearing your new outfit. You like it a great deal and are pleased when your friend says that she thinks it is terrific. You say

   a) Thanks, I'm glad you like it, because I really do.

   b) Oh this! It's nothing special.

   c) Oh! I . . . got it on sale—it was cheap.

2. Your secretary has begun to produce letters badly with a lot of typing errors. You say

   a) Your work's been terrible this week. What's wrong with you?

   b) I've been surprised by your work this week. There have been a lot of typing errors. Can we talk about it?

   c) These letters are really not good enough. You're getting careless—or lazy.

3. A colleague asks to borrow your car. You would rather not loan your car to him. You say

   a) Well . . . okay . . . I suppose it's all right.

   b) You've got nerve. Of course you can't. Borrow someone else's car.

   c) I'd rather not. I'm very possessive about my car. It might seem odd, but I'd still rather not.

4. You would like your friend to pick up a newspaper for you on his way to your house. You say

   a) Would you mind picking up an evening paper on your way over here? I'd really appreciate it.

   b) I don't suppose you're passing a . . . oh, never mind, it's not important.

   c) I really want a paper, but I don't have time to get it myself.

5. You met a person yesterday who you like very much and you would like to go out with her. You see her again the next day and say

   a) I'd really like to go out with you. How about Saturday?

   b) Well, what are you doing with yourself these days?

   c) I hear there's a good film at the Odeon this week.

6. You are taking a defective record back to the store. The salesperson says it must be your fault. You know that it was damaged when you first played it. You say

   a) It sounded like this the first time I played it. I don't see how it can be my fault. I would like a new one.

   b) Don't be ridiculous. I wouldn't try to trick you. Are you calling me a liar?

   c) Oh, all right.

7. Equipment is in very short supply in your department. You have bought some pens for yourself and have put them in your office. A junior colleague comes in, picks them up, and walks off. You say

   a) Excuse me . . . oh . . . (under your breath) well, she's young . . . it's not her fault . . . .

   b) I'm sorry, but those pens are mine. I really shouldn't have put them down there.

   c) Those pens are mine. I would like them back.

Answers

1. a) Assertive

   You are pleased that someone likes it and you accept the compliment.

   b) Unassertive

   You are embarrassed at the compliment and try to negate it.

   c) Unassertive

   You are embarrassed at the compliment and try to negate it.

2. a) Aggressive

   You launch an attack with no consideration of a previously high standard.

   b) Assertive

   You acknowledge previous good work, state your dissatisfaction clearly, and invite comment.

   c) Aggressive

   You make unhelpful, critical comments.

3. a) Unassertive

   You will most likely feel bad later, or angry at your colleague for asking you. Your colleague is being assertive. You are not.

   b) Aggressive

   You can refuse without putting him down.

   c) Assertive

   Your colleague might not like it, but that's the way you are. He knows where he stands, and he also knows that, in the future, you can be relied on to be honest and straightforward.

4. a) Assertive

   Your friend always has the right to refuse.

b) Unassertive

Assume that your friend will refuse if it is inconvenient. If he will not, then it is about time he learned to be assertive!

c) Unassertive

You are trying to manipulate your friend into offering. He may not be aware of your intentions or may be annoyed that you are being devious.

5. a) Assertive

b) Unassertive.

You are backing off from asking for what you really want. The likelihood is that you will not get it.

c) Unassertive

Your message is not clear. She has to guess what you really want. If she wants it also, it puts her in a difficult situation. She might worry that she is wrong and so may not be assertive enough to take the risk of following it up. You are basically trying to manipulate her to ask you!

6. a) Assertive

You are standing up for your rights. You know you are not to blame and you have the right as a consumer to get satisfaction. You are not angry with the salesperson because the fault is in the manufacturing.

b) Aggressive

You will either frighten or annoy the salesperson. If frightened, the salesperson feels walked on; if you anger the salesperson, you are less likely to get cooperation.

c) Unassertive

You are being walked on.

7. a) Unassertive

Don't you want your pens?

b) Unassertive.

There's no need to apologize. Your apologetic manner may make your colleague embarrassed.

c) Assertive

A quick, straightforward (smiling) response defuses a potentially awkward situation.

How did you do in gauging the different responses? In the space below, write down any learning points that you picked up as a result of this activity.

Assertive, Aggressive, and Unassertive Behavior

ASSERTIVE	
You Do	**You Don't**
• Ask for what you want	• Violate other people's rights
• Speak directly and openly	• Expect other people to guess what you want
• Respond appropriately	• Freeze up with anxiety
• Have rights	
• Ask confidently and without undue anxiety	
AGGRESSIVE	
You Do	**You Don't**
• Try to get what you want	• Respect that other people have a right to have their needs met
• Respond in whatever way works	• Look for situations in which you both might be able to get what you want ("win-win situations")
• Often cause bad feelings in others	
• Threaten, cajole, manipulate, use sarcasm, fight	
UNASSERTIVE	
You Do	**You Don't**
• Hope that you will get what you want	• Ask for what you want
• Stifle your feelings	• Express your feelings
• Rely on others to guess what you want	• Usually get what you want
	• Upset anyone
	• Get noticed

Describe a recent situation where your response was not assertive.

The situation

_____

_____

I said

_____

_____

What I should have said

_____

_____

Personal Project

It is important to begin to put into practice what you are reading about. Over the next few days, watch for situations where you are asked to do something that you don't necessarily want to do, but that you would normally agree to anyway. When you see this beginning to happen, instead of saying "yes," say "no," using the assertive manner that was described in our quiz. (You might have noticed that assertive refusals don't usually include the word "no!") Return to this page after completing the project and fill in the spaces below.

I felt

_____

_____

S/he said

_____

_____

In the end

_____

_____

Summary

The quiz gave you different responses for a wide range of situations from the classic scenario of returning merchandise to asking a small favor. We hope you remembered (from Chapter 1) that how you stand, your tone of voice, and the expression on your face all contribute to the overall impression you make. Note that, in the last question, the assertive response could sound aggressive if you had a sharp, unsmiling tone. Begin to practice more assertive behavior.

3

You
Have
Rights

W e talked in the last chapter about your personal rights and responsibilities. You cannot change your behavior without also having an effect on others—an effect they may not like, or that might take some getting used to. Therefore, it's important to be aware of both your rights and your responsibilities to others.

All human beings have rights. We're entitled to them by virtue of our very existence. In 1948, the United Nations proclaimed 30 Articles as a Universal Declaration of Human Rights. They cover broad and very basic issues: the right to life, liberty, a home, education, health, etc. Only a few of them have been achieved worldwide, but they exist as a benchmark for humankind.

Experts on psychology and how the human mind grows and develops say that in our relationships with other people we are bound to have expectations of them. Just as children expect parents to look after them, so we have expectations in our relationships. We expect our friends to behave considerately. We have a right to such reasonable expectations. We do not have a right to unreasonable expectations such as a person giving up a cherished pastime for us! What is reasonable and unreasonable is a matter of judgment for each of us, but by allowing others the same rights as we expect for ourselves, we can be fairly sure that our expectations of one another will be reasonable.

The Rights that we list next may seem quite ordinary and acceptable when you first read them, but it can take a long time for some of these rights to sink in—for you to accept them for yourself as well as for other people. Read the list carefully and sign it: These are your rights and you are entitled to them. It helps to read them through often; for example, at times when you feel assailed by doubts over the rights and wrongs of your assertive behavior.

Try reading the list aloud to yourself.

My Rights

1. I have the right to ask for what I want (recognizing that other people have the right to say no).
2. I have the right to have my own opinions and values and to express them appropriately.
3. I have the right to change my mind.
4. I have the right to make my own decisions and to deal with the consequences.
5. I have the right to decline responsibility for other people's problems.
6. I have the right to be successful.
7. I have the right to privacy, to be alone, and to be independent.
8. I have the right to say "I don't know" and "I don't understand."
9. I have the right to change myself and to be an assertive person.
10. I have the right to say "No" and "Yes" without feeling guilty.
11. I have the right to relate to others without being dependent on them for approval.

Signed

_____

Date

_____

Did you read the list aloud? Did you sign the declaration? How do you feel about these eleven statements?

_____

_____

_____

Many people have little difficulty in accepting these rights for others, but the way they lead their own lives shows that they do not accept them for themselves.

We can be overly tolerant and quick to make excuses for others:

- "Well, he'll know better next time."
- "You're only young once."
- "She probably didn't understand."

But we don't always make those same excuses for ourselves!

- "I'm 40 years old. You'd think I'd have learned by now."
- "I should have kept my big mouth shut."
- "I'm so stupid. I never get anything right the first time."

Look again at "My Rights" and decide if you feel comfortable with each one, or if there are ways in which you don't give yourself the degree of respect to which you are entitled. Write down any thoughts you have about the rights to personalize them.

My Thoughts

1. _____

2. _____

3. _____

4. _____

5. _____

6. _____

7. _____

8. _____

9. _____

10. _____

11. _____

What have you written down? Are you happy that your annotated list of rights reflects the way you feel about yourself? Or are you worried and secretly afraid that perhaps you don't have the right to privacy, or the right to say "No"? It can certainly seem that way at times—when you're caring for young children, for example, it is practically impossible to get any privacy or time to yourself. Using this as an example, think of two ways you could make time for some privacy without abandoning family, friends, or colleagues and their needs:

1. _____

2. _____

A Few Words on Responsibility

This example shows clearly that each of these personal rights has its accompanying responsibility. First and foremost, you are responsible for the welfare of your children, family, or colleagues—to see that their needs are met. But you also have a responsibility to yourself—to make the decision and the arrangements for your privacy. We only achieve our rights when we shoulder the accompanying responsibility—and when we do, we become stronger, more capable of being proactive, and more in control of our own lives.

What other responsibilities can you see arising from this list of rights?

_____

_____

_____

_____

_____

The list of rights becomes less daunting when you realize that it works both ways: if you can say "No" to others, they also can say "No" to you. Having the right, in effect, gives you the responsibility of choice. For example, the right to decline responsibility for other people's problems may seem uncaring until you recognize that having the right is not the same as always declining responsibility for other people's problems. But for those of us who give in again and again to the sometimes selfish demands of others, this right gives us the choice of declining without feeling guilty. We are then in a position to make responsible choices instead of being manipulated by others.

Rather than giving a list of responsibilities that go along with these rights, perhaps we can simply say

I have a responsibility to give these rights to myself and to others.

Summary

This chapter has outlined the rights and responsibilities of an assertive person. While it may be difficult at first to accept that you have these rights, not doing so can lead to passive behavior. Not expecting others to accord you these rights can allow them to behave aggressively toward you.

You may need to return to this chapter and read it again, or to remind yourself of your rights from time to time, before you can begin fully to accept your own ability to allow these rights to yourself and to other people.

4

Being
Assertive

You have already learned a lot about assertiveness, but have you started to put it into practice yet? Let's take a minute to see where you are now. The following questionnaires will help you to measure how assertive you are in your work and in your home life. You can fill out one or both questionnaires—using both will enable you to make comparisons such as "am I more assertive at home or at work?"

How Assertive Am I at Work?

AT WORK I FIND IT EASIER WITH:	PEOPLE "SENIOR" TO ME	PEOPLE "JUNIOR" TO ME	OTHER COLLEAGUES	YOUNGER PEOPLE	SUPPORT STAFF	OTHERS
To Express Positive Feelings By:						
• Telling them that I appreciate them						
• Giving praise/ compliments						
• Receiving praise openly and without embarrassment						
• Making requests						
• Starting conversations						
Directions: Mark ✓ for Usually, X for Seldom.						

AT WORK I FIND IT EASIER WITH:	PEOPLE "SENIOR" TO ME	PEOPLE "JUNIOR" TO ME	OTHER COLLEAGUES	YOUNGER PEOPLE	SUPPORT STAFF	OTHERS
To Express Negative Feelings By:						
• Showing annoyance						
• Showing I feel hurt						
Directions: Mark ✓ for Usually, X for Seldom.						

AT WORK I FIND IT EASIER WITH:	PEOPLE "SENIOR" TO ME	PEOPLE "JUNIOR" TO ME	OTHER COLLEAGUES	YOUNGER PEOPLE	SUPPORT STAFF	OTHERS
To Stand Up for My Rights By:						
• Refusing requests						
• Refusing to be "put down"						
• Offering my opinion						
• Making suggestions						
Directions: Mark ✓ for Usually, X for Seldom.						

Who is it easiest to be assertive with?

_____

Why do you think so?

_____

_____

_____

Who is it hardest to be assertive with?

_____

Why do you think so?

_____

_____

_____

How Assertive Am I at Home?

AT HOME I FIND IT EASIER WITH:	PARTNER	FRIENDS	PARENTS/ CHILDREN	OTHER RELATIVES	PEOPLE IN AUTHORITY	PEOPLE WHO PROVIDE SERVICES
To Express Positive Feelings By:						
• Telling them that I appreciate them						
• Giving praise/ compliments						
• Receiving praise openly and without embarrassment						
• Making requests						
• Starting conversations						
Directions: Mark ✓ for Usually, X for Seldom.						

AT HOME I FIND IT EASIER WITH:	PARTNER	FRIENDS	PARENTS/ CHILDREN	OTHER RELATIVES	PEOPLE IN AUTHORITY	PEOPLE WHO PROVIDE SERVICES
To Express Negative Feelings By:						
• Showing Annoyance						
• Showing I feel hurt						
Directions: Mark ✓ for Usually, X for Seldom.						

AT HOME I FIND IT EASIER WITH:	PARTNER	FRIENDS	PARENTS/ CHILDREN	OTHER RELATIVES	PEOPLE IN AUTHORITY	PEOPLE WHO PROVIDE SERVICES
To Stand Up for My Rights By:						
• Refusing requests						
• Refusing to be "put down"						
• Offering my opinion						
• Making complaints						
Directions: Mark ✓ for Usually, X for Seldom.						

Who is it easiest to be assertive with?

_____

Why do you think so?

_____

_____

_____

Who is it hardest to be assertive with?

_____

Why do you think so?

_____

_____

_____

Now that you've completed the questionnaires, look at your ✓'s and x's. In the space below, write down three things you're pleased with, and three things you'd like to change.

I'm pleased with

1. _____
2. _____
3. _____

I'd like to change

1. _____
2. _____
3. _____

Congratulate yourself on the positives! Make a note here of how you will change the areas you're not happy with.

I will

_____

_____

When?

_____

_____

Assertive Behavior at Work

Assertive behavior in the workplace gives everyone a better chance of influencing the system and participating in changes. Relationships are more open and working environments are more genuine. Overtly aggressive or manipulative behavior can (as we said in Chapter 1) bring immediate results, but credibility and integrity are put at risk. When people feel defensive and have to use their energy for political maneuvering, everyone in the organization suffers.

People behaving assertively make good line managers. They will say clearly what they want, be equally supportive of staff, and take the needs of others into account. They can compromise and negotiate.

The introduction of assertive behavior into the workplace, whether it be a school, an office, or shop floor, will probably involve an intense transition period. Expressing negative feelings or standing up for individual rights can be interpreted as out of order or insubordinate.

Assertive behavior is so important to self-esteem and proactive behavior that it needs to be particularly supported and endorsed in young workers or school children and students. If you work with young people as a teacher or employer, we hope that you will encourage them to develop these skills.

Differences

We believe that the completed questionnaires will look very different, according to whether you are female or male. In many societies, women tend to be passive while men are often aggressive. You'll also respond differently if you are from a minority ethnic group.

Women may have difficulty with

- Expressing anger
- Being assertive (rather than manipulative)
- Dealing with authority figures
- Being an authority figure

Men may have difficulty with

- Talking about vulnerability or weakness
- Talking about errors they've made
- Women authority figures

Appropriate Assertiveness

Now let's look at the questionnaires in light of *appropriate behavior*. Remember two of the points we made about appropriateness in Chapter 1? Assertive behavior is suitable or appropriate for the occasion. Appropriate assertive behavior allows you to express your feelings without offending others.

If you consider the people and the behaviors on your questionnaires, you will realize that with some people and in some situations, assertive behavior won't work.

Looking back at the answers to your questionnaires, think of three types of situations where assertiveness may not work, or three kinds of people it doesn't work with.

1. _____

2. _____

3. _____

Do these three examples have anything in common?

_____

How can you deal with these situations?

_____

_____

In these situations we still have choices, depending on who the people are and how they are behaving. If they are behaving aggressively, we can either respond in kind, or we can continue to behave assertively (and fairly) in the hope they will learn from our example. The latter would provide a better role model for children, but what about the person in authority? In this case, remember your rights, particularly your right to decline responsibility for another's problems. Make an assertive choice not to get involved in a confrontation—you have the right to steer your own course.

Remember that being assertive may not always be the most effective way of getting what you want with some people—especially people who are not assertive themselves.

Consider again the behaviors from the questionnaires on pages 36-39. Check those that seem to be the most socially acceptable to you.

	Check here
1. Express appreciation.	☐
2. Give praise and compliments.	☐
3. Receive praise with pleasure.	☐
4. Make requests.	☐
5. Initiate conversations.	☐
6. Show annoyance.	☐
7. Show hurt feelings.	☐
8. Refuse requests.	☐
9. Refuse to be put down.	☐
10. Offer comments and opinions.	☐
11. Make complaints.	☐

We suggest check marks beside numbers 1 to 5. Numbers 6 and 7, while they may be valid expressions of feeling on occasion, are not usually socially acceptable, and numbers 8 to 11 are about our rights, which may sometimes conflict with the perceived or expressed needs of other people. This is why appropriateness is so important.

From this list, it is clear that being assertive about negative feelings and standing up for our rights tend to be less socially acceptable than expressing positive feelings.

We have to be very careful before we launch ourselves on everyone we know to display our new assertiveness! It could be counterproductive.

Increase Assertiveness by Expressing More Positive Feelings First

People will be more prepared to listen to negative feelings, or to our requests for our rights, if we've made positive remarks about them first. Select someone from the questionnaire to whom you want or may need to say something negative. What can you say first that's positive to him/her?

_____

_____

Is there anyone else, in either the "Negative" section or the "Rights" section, to whom you can also find something positive to say?

_____

If your manager needed to say something negative or critical to you, what positive thing would you like him or her to say first?

_____

_____

Summary

From these questionnaires you will discover or clarify more about yourself as an assertive person, and you will note areas that you need to work on. We briefly looked at assertive behavior in the workplace and acknowledged the differences that race and gender make.

We looked at appropriateness as a vital social skill and adjunct to assertive behavior. We noted that

- Some people will not like assertive behavior, because it is not in their best interest.
- We need to behave appropriately with different people; for example, with parents or an employer.
- We can begin to be more assertive by expressing our positive feelings about people first. They may then be more receptive to negative feelings.

Write down here your two *main* learning points from this chapter.

1. _____

2. _____

5

How to
Be Assertive

The Skills So Far

This section summarizes the skills we have already examined and asks you to plan when and how you will put them into practice. This advance planning will make it easier for you when you're ready to try out what you have learned.

1. *Know What You Want:* You won't appear confident if you are unsure of what you want. You could seem foolish by asking for something that you eventually decide is not what you want.

2. *Say It:* Don't hesitate or beat around the bush, come right out with it! Practice what you want to say before you say it to check for appropriateness.

3. *Be Specific:* Say exactly what you want or do not want, so that there can be no confusion. Long explanations are unnecessary.Begin with the word "I."

4. *Say What You Have to Say as Soon as Possible:* Do not let too much time pass, as this builds up apprehension. On the other hand, do not say anything at the peak of your anger; wait for it to pass.

5. *Look the Person in the Eye:* People feel more comfortable if you look directly at them. You look shifty if you cannot look them in the eye. You certainly will not come across as being confident about what you want.

6. *Look Relaxed:* You'll convey anxiety by fidgeting or waving your arms around; or conversely, by being too rigid. Practice looking relaxed in a mirror—it's not as contradictory as it sounds!

7. *Avoid Laughing Nervously:* Smile if it's appropriate, but if you giggle or laugh you won't come across as if you mean what you say. You'll confuse the person you are speaking to.

8. *Don't Whine or Be Sarcastic:* Be direct and honest. Whining and pleading can either annoy the person or

make him or her feel guilty. It is being manipulative. Being sarcastic, on the other hand, communicates hostility as you put the other person down.

> Note here the skills that you feel reasonably confident about, and think you can use.

Now you have to practice all these dimensions of assertive behavior—and put together all the different components of the positive process. We suggest that you look again at the questionnaire you completed in Chapter 4. Is there a "people" column and a "situations" row with quite a number of X's in it? Now take a few minutes to complete the following, using people and situations from the questionnaires. Take your time and visualize the scenario as you complete the spaces below.

The situation is

_____

_____

1. Know what you want to say.

What I want to say to

_____

Is:

_____

_____

_____

2. Say it!

The sentence I will use is

_____

_____

_____

_____

3. Be specific.

Check your first sentence; if it is not crystal clear, you might have to repeat the statement more clearly, being more specific. How might you reword it, starting with the word "I"? Concentrate on exactly what you want out of the situation.

_____

_____

_____

4. Say it as soon as possible.

Choose your time and place appropriately: It may not be a good idea to grab someone in the corridor at work, or to interrupt when someone is busy. Choose a setting that will help you feel at ease and that will allow you to use the body language we have discussed—but don't put if off!

The conversation will take place at (time)

_____

_____

In (location)

_____

5. Look the person in the eye.
6. Look relaxed.
7. No nervous laughing.

Imagine the setting you have chosen and how you will be sitting or standing. Imagine you are facing the person. Practice your sentence (numbers 2 and 3 above) out loud. Look at yourself in the mirror—don't laugh! How does it feel? What will you do if the person takes no notice?

8. Don't whine or be sarcastic.

If your response tends toward this, make a note here of how you can change this, bearing in mind the information on body language and tone of voice you already have read about.

Summary

In this chapter, we have expanded on what you actually need to do to be more assertive, listing the skills and giving you an opportunity to visualize putting them into practice.

Having visualized the scene will put you more in command of yourself. But of course you cannot control the other person and must accept that some people cannot handle your assertiveness.

If this happens, don't be disappointed; there are several ways of handling it. First, if this is the kind of person with whom assertiveness makes no difference, then try an easier situation for yourself. Visualize it again—and then try it. Practice in the easier situations will build your confidence for dealing with people who cannot cope with assertive behavior. Introduce yourself (and others) gently to your new assertive skills.

Finally, the next chapters will provide you with some additional skills for dealing with really uncompromising people and difficult situations. Read on!

6

Skill Sharpening

I n this chapter we tell you more of the fundamental skills of assertive behavior and suggest ways that you can practice them. Changing behavior isn't easy and, if you are moving from being unassertive to being more aware of your needs and rights, other people who just want a handy doormat will initially be resistant to any changes in you!

Broken Record

We will look first at the skill of being persistent (sometimes called Broken Record). This is the skill of repeating over and over what you want or need until you achieve it or can negotiate. Being persistent won't lead to great intellectual debate; in fact, it can be really irritating to the other people involved, but it's very useful when your time and your energy are valuable to you (which is most of the time!).

For example:

- When you want to get children to bed
- When you don't want to work late to help out a colleague
- When you have faulty merchandise to return to a store

Now take one incident in your own daily life (simple ones are best to start with) where you'd like to be persistent and write it down here.

_____

_____

Now write down one or two clear, straightforward sentences that will help you respond to the situation.

_____

_____

Rehearse these sentences. Say them several times. Look at yourself in a mirror, remembering what you learned in Chapter 1 about body language.

When you have practiced a sentence, slightly altering the words so that they don't sound too contrived, practice using it together with a sentence that *empathizes* with the other person. (This shows that you're aware that the other person has a problem as well, even though you are not going to resolve it.)

You could try to role-play the situation with a friend. Explain the situation so that your friend can take the part of the other person; he or she can keep coming back at you, trying to get you to change your mind. You can keep repeating the same basic point, in slightly different ways, until you get the message across. The following example will give you the idea. While you're reading it, look for the ways that Martin tries to wheedle and put pressure on Roger. Note how Roger handles this by repeating the same message in different ways—and how he shows some empathy for Martin's problem while refusing to take it on himself.

Martin (4:30 p.m.):	"I've got to leave early today and the boss has just given me this report. Can you finish it for me? It shouldn't take you too long."
Roger:	"I'd like to help you, but I want to leave on time myself today."
Martin:	"But I promised I'd meet someone—that girl, Natalie. Are you doing anything else tonight?"
Roger:	"I really want to leave on time myself tonight."
Martin:	"Well, I don't know Rog, you always seem to be hanging around—I thought you liked to help out."
Roger:	"Yes, I do like to help out, but tonight I want to leave on time."

A few minutes later, Martin departs to ask someone else.

Are there any points about this "conversation" that you thought were significant?

_____

_____

_____

You might have noted that

- It's tedious to be on the receiving end of someone being a Broken Record!
- Roger didn't let himself be side-tracked at all; he didn't say whether he was, or wasn't, doing anything else that evening. It wasn't relevant to the fact that he didn't want to work late. He kept to the point.
- Roger acknowledged the truth of Martin's slight "dig" about helping out, but immediately returned to the Broken Record.
- Roger used very little energy compared to either arguing with Martin or "giving in" and feeling downtrodden (which uses tremendous amounts of energy).

The Broken Record can be useful in a meeting—the kind where misleading clues are constantly used to divert attention. Subtle persistence can bring the attention of the meeting back to the subject you want.

Managing the Putdown

The second skill we introduce you to in this section is how to manage the putdown (or, if you prefer a more technical description of this behavior—stopping manipulative criticism and protecting your self-esteem).

Did you notice the attempt at a putdown or a diversionary side-step in the conversation between Roger and Martin? Martin said to Roger that he always seemed to be hanging around—"I thought you liked to help out." Roger could have replied indignantly, "I don't hang around, what are you talking about—I'm just very hard-working—unlike some people!" If he had said that, the conversation would have taken a very different turn and Roger would undoubtedly have come out of it feeling exhausted and defeated.

Recognizing the Putdown

Sometimes people try to boost their own poor self-esteem by knocking down ours; sometimes the putdown is well disguised as a joke or as a conversational reply. At other times it is more blatant. Does all this seem a little like a war zone? You may think that people don't really behave like this, but look at the following list of putdowns. Are any familiar?

"You're just like your mother."
"When you're my age . . ."
"I know I can count on you . . ."
"Typical woman."
"Come on, it's only in fun . . ."
"You look beautiful when you're angry . . ."
"You (whatever) are all the same . . ."

The trouble with putdowns is that you don't always recognize them immediately, but after the conversation is over you might think to yourself, "What did he or she mean by that?" This after-effect needlessly reawakens your private fears and doubts about yourself.

Sometimes a putdown is disguised as a compliment: "Michael's got a great sense of humor—it's a laugh a minute with him" or "How nice to be young and irresponsible." It's a no-win situation: If you do ask the speaker what is meant by the remark, you may well be put off with "It was only a joke. Why do you take everything so personally?" This is, in effect, a double putdown because it now suggests that not only are you stupid and irresponsible but also that you are overly sensitive!

Can you think of one or two phrases that you have said to someone, or maybe had said to you, that would fall into this category?

_____

_____

_____

_____

Dealing With the Putdown

The temptation for us all is to think of brilliant, cutting remarks that we could have made in reply. But after the event has passed, we are just wasting our mental energy on a self-recrimination like, "Why didn't I think of to say that at the time?" Even if you could think up your own putdown at the time, this is simply falling into the trap of aggressive behavior and is ultimately counterproductive for both you and the other person.

If this is happening to you and you cannot manage an assertive reply at the time, don't worry! When you have had time to think it over, you can take the person aside and tell him or her assertively how you feel about the remark. Remembering your list of Rights will help you, as will the techniques of Negative Inquiry and Fogging, which follow.

Here is a short list of familiar putdowns; there is a hidden message and an assertive response to each.

The Putdown	The Hidden Message	You Say
If I were you . . .	I'm smarter than you!	But you're not me!
If only you'd cooperate . . .	You have to fall into line with me.	How can we cooperate?
You're not going to like this . . .	I'm going to make you tense/angry before I say more . . .	I'll choose my own response.
That will be difficult for you because you can be a bit bossy . . .	I have the right to give you criticism you didn't ask for.	In what ways do you think I'm bossy?

Negative Inquiry

You probably noticed that in the fourth putdown the response was in the form of a question. This is called Negative Inquiry. You actively seek criticism of your behavior—but only if you're prepared for a straight answer. (Sometimes it's helpful to ask for criticism, but that's another whole book in itself!) If your critic wasn't sincere, then your question will be put off: "Oh, I didn't mean it" or "Oh, just my little joke."

Are you getting the idea? Write your own response to these situations.

The Putdown	The Hidden Message	You Say
Are you busy tonight?	Got you! Your time is not as valuable as mine . . .	
I know I'm being nosey, but . . .	I have more rights than you . . .	

For the first one we hope you suggested something like: "What did you have in mind?" This is a bit like Negative Inquiry; it does not seeking criticism, but it definitely calls their bluff!

For the second one, you might have suggested: "Well, I won't tell you if I don't want to." The other person hides their putdown of you by pretending to put his or her own self down! Don't be drawn into this game; make your position clear. You have the right to choose whether to tell or not, once you know what it is that is so important to find out.

Fogging

This is a useful technique to use when the putdown has some truth in it but has been exaggerated. For example: "Your desk is a real mess. It gives a really bad impression of the whole department. It's typical of your attitude."

If there is truth in the accusation, your assertive response is to accept the grain of truth—but not the putdown. You could say "Yes. My desk is a mess. I'll straighten it up today."

You don't need to respond to the criticism about your attitude with protestations about how hard you work, though you could say "Yes. My desk is a mess—I've been busy. I'll straighten it up today."

Can you note here three criticisms that people make of you, or that you are concerned might be made about you? What response, using Fogging or Negative Inquiry, could be made to each of them?

Criticism	Response
1._____	1._____
2._____	2._____
3._____	3._____

Summary

In this chapter, we have looked at skill sharpening techniques. We looked at the important skill of persistence (Broken Record) to use when time and energy are valuable or we when don't want to become too involved in a situation. We then went on to look at a number of general examples of how to recognize and handle manipulative criticism and attacks to self-esteem. We then had a brief look at Negative Inquiry and Fogging as counters to a putdown.

Can you note here two learning points for you from this chapter?

1. _____

2. _____

What action can you take on what you've just written?

1. _____

2. _____

When will you take this action?

_____

7

Criticism
and
Compliments

Most of us find it very difficult to accept criticism, and it can be just as hard when you have to offer it. Often this stems from our childhood experience of criticism, which may have been accompanied by feelings of blame, guilt, and fear of rejection. Even as adults, we still experience criticism as withdrawal of approval, affection, and esteem. It hurts!

The first way to take the sting out of criticism is to distinguish between valid and invalid criticism.

Valid Criticism

Valid criticism is criticism that you know to be fair because you really did arrive late or forget your papers, or you weren't listening, or you really have been irritable or impatient lately. In this case, learn to accept that the criticism is valid and that it only criticizes one aspect of your behavior—it does not reject you as a person.

Allow yourself to accept the truth of the criticism by agreeing openly with it. You do not have to run and hide, find excuses, or apologize for mistakes; just agree in the most simple and direct way possible.

What responses could you make in answer to the criticisms cited above? Write them down here, be as direct as possible, and do not put yourself down in the process.

_____

_____

_____

_____

_____

We thought of responses like

"Yes. I know I'm sometimes forgetful."

"I'm sorry I'm late."

"I'm sorry; I was daydreaming. You're right, I wasn't listening."

"I apologize for being so irritable lately."

It is important to say the words "forgetful" or "late" or "not listening" even though you may be reluctant to admit to your faults at first. By saying the words, you will reduce their importance from that of unmentionable horror to a small, easily acceptable fact.

Invalid Criticism

Invalid criticism is defined as any criticism that is simply untrue or meant to put you down. Sometimes it is difficult to recognize whether criticism is valid or invalid; for instance, someone may accuse you of being lazy. You may think you are hard working, but then you remember the occasions when you have been lazy, so you accept the criticism, even though you feel you have been unfairly criticized. You have to ask yourself if this criticism is generally true of you—do you "own" it? If not, you can assertively refuse to own an unfair generalization:

"That's not really true! I am generally very hard working!"

or

"That's not fair. It's unreasonable to focus on one instance, when I generally work very hard."

Receiving Criticism

In the previous chapter, you drew up a short list of criticisms that people have made of you or that you are afraid people might make. Expand this list and divide it into valid and invalid criticisms. Write down five criticisms, and be sure you put only criticisms that you "own" and accept as true in the Valid column.

Valid	Invalid
1. _____	_____
2. _____	_____
3. _____	_____
4. _____	_____
5. _____	_____

The next exercise will help you cope with the next time you are on the receiving end of criticism. You can do it alone or with a friend. If you are with a friend, give the list to him or her so you may be given both valid and invalid criticisms. You can practice the techniques out loud of accepting and assertively rejecting the criticisms. Alternatively, imagine someone making these criticisms of you. Hear his or her exact words in your mind; visualize the scene where the person is sitting or standing, how he or she looks at you, and so on—and then reply clearly and firmly.

Remember to use assertive body language and tone of voice, as well as assertive wording. If it helps you to work it out in advance, you can use the following space to write down the exact criticisms and your replies

Criticism:

_____

Your reply:

_____

_____

Criticism:

_____

Your reply:

_____

_____

Criticism:

_____

Your reply:

_____

_____

Criticism:

_____

Your reply:

_____

_____

Remember that valid criticism applies to only one aspect of your behavior and not to you as a person. Now let's restore the balance by looking at some positive aspects of your behavior. Use this space to write down five positive things about yourself.

1. _____

2. _____

3. _____

4. _____

5. _____

Remember that giving or receiving invalid criticism (especially putdowns) lowers our self-esteem, unless we find effective techniques of rejecting it. Read over your list of five good things again. And again. You don't need to put other people down, nor should you let other people do it to you.

So how do you give criticism in a way that is constructive and not hurtful?

Giving Criticism

We hope that reminding yourself of your good points will take the sting out of your criticisms of yourself. Remember that the same principle applies to times when you have to criticize others.

- Try to say something positive about the person first. This is one way we can make our criticism more constructive and easier for the person to accept. Say "I'm very pleased with the quality of your work, and your attitude is very good, but you can't wear jeans in the office."

- Be even-handed. Give praise where you can. This helps the recipient remember that his or her good points are valued by you, so your criticism can be accepted without loss of self-esteem.

- Make sure your criticism refers to specific behavior and does not label the whole person. For example, compare "You're such a slob, your room is always a mess!" with "I see you haven't straightened your room yet. Could you do it now?"

- Make a clear, constructive suggestion as to what you'd like done. Vague hints about what you would like are no help to the other person, so make your request specific, such as: "Thank you for the report. It looks great. However, your desk is a terrible mess. Please take some time to straighten it up."

- Express your feelings honestly. Do not assume that a person is aware of the effect his or her behavior is having on you. Avoid angry scenes, choose your time and place, and state your feelings calmly and without hostility. For example "When you interrupt me like that I feel as though what I am saying is not important. Please try not to do it again."

Think of a criticism you have made, or would like to make, of someone. Is it a valid criticism? How can you apply the techniques described above to ensure your criticism is made in a way that is not aggressive but constructive and friendly so it will be easier for the person to accept? Write down one or two suggestions here.

_____

_____

_____

_____

A Few More Words on Giving and Receiving Criticism

There are some subjects that we feel strongly about, and we cannot help reacting badly if someone criticizes us on those points. Often it is something very personal that others are unaware we feel sensitive about, such as the size of our nose, our weight or height, our education, our race, or our religion. We all have them—our sensitive spots. The only way to make this sort of personal criticism from others more bearable is by the method you practiced above: by accepting the criticism and saying the actual words to "take the heat" out of your feelings.

If someone else has remarked on one of these sensitive spots, the chances are that it is accidental, that he or she has no idea of the effect it might have on you. This is when you need to state your feelings. Or the person may be aware of your sensitivity and is attempting a putdown. In any case, you should be able to deal better with those situations now, having done the exercises in this book.

Finally, remember the value of praise in restoring someone's self-esteem. Particularly after a long or difficult discussion, when perhaps there has been criticism on both sides, remember how valuable and important it can be to be reminded of the other's good points: It restores confidence in the relationship. Always try to end on a positive note, like "I'm glad we've had this chance to talk things through. I really value your opinions."

Giving and Receiving Compliments

To some extent we have already touched on this subject, and you should already have an appreciation of the importance of giving compliments or "positive feedback" in enhancing people's sense of self-worth. So, why don't we accept compliments more readily, when we know how good they make us feel? Take some time now to write down your thoughts on this.

_____

_____

_____

_____

Perhaps you included reasons such as: "because we were told as children not to be vain or boastful about our talents," or "because it is embarrassing." When someone says you are clever, you feel as if he or she has discovered that you secretly aspire to cleverness. Or maybe you feel that people only pay you a compliment when they want something; their compliment isn't true.

These are all defensive reactions—we don't want to believe what they say. It is true that people sometimes give compliments to try to manipulate you. As with criticism, the main art here is to distinguish between the genuine and the fake compliment. You can do this the same way as you did with valid and invalid criticism: Ask yourself, "Is it true? Am I able to accept and own this praise?" If you know perfectly well that the compliment refers to something you are proud of and like about yourself, or if the compliment is because of something you have been working very hard at, then accept it! You deserve it!

Accepting Compliments

False modesty not only belittles your abilities, it makes a fool of the person doing the complimenting, and it can be very annoying. So avoid a brush-off such as "It was nothing" or "I'm not very good at it really." Accept the compliment gracefully—or better still, assertively. Try this:

"Thank you for the compliment. I have been working really hard at losing weight. I'm glad you noticed it."

"I'm glad you liked the meal. I like trying new recipes."

"Yes. I worked very hard to produce a really good report. It's great to know I succeeded."

Look now at your list of five positive things about yourself. Is there anything you want to add? If you can, do this exercise with a friend. Exchange lists and practice giving and receiving compliments. If you are doing it alone, visualize who will make the compliment, what he or she will say, how, and where. Practice this aloud, visualizing how you will sit or stand and how you will look as you say the exact words you will use to accept the compliment assertively. If you want to prepare what it is you want to say, use this space.

_____

_____

_____

As with giving and receiving criticism, using the specific words takes some of the heat, or embarrassment, out of the situation. If you can also follow up by showing your feelings of pleasure at receiving such a compliment, so much the better—it lets the other person know his or her remarks are valued. What kind of facial expression will you use? We hope you answered: a smile.

Giving Compliments

We often take people for granted, especially those we care about most. We assume that they must know how we feel, that they are clever, and that we admire their abilities. But the previous exercises we have done show that you cannot expect people to know these things unless you tell them; and the more simple, clear, and direct you can be, the better. So the first golden rule is

- Express your feelings positively and assertively.

By now you know that "assertively" does not mean getting carried away! Gushing "I think you are wonderful" is vague, too unspecific to be helpful, and reeks of gratuitous flattery. Always remember to

- Keep it simple.
- Be specific about what it is you are complimenting.

- Be clear and confident of your right to express your opinions.
- Be honest.

Now think of five compliments that you would like to give but have always felt too shy or embarrassed to say. Remember the good effect that accepting compliments naturally and easily had on you, and the good effect it has on relationships. Even bosses like to receive recognition of a job well done!

1. _____
2. _____
3. _____
4. _____
5. _____

And Finally

With time, you will see that giving and receiving compliments will become as natural and easy as giving someone a smile. And you will find the rewards of being able to express your feelings clearly and directly in this way far outweigh the time and effort taken to read this book and do the exercises.

Summary

In this chapter we have concentrated on how techniques of assertiveness can be applied to giving and receiving compliments and criticism. We hope that, through continued practice, you can build on the skills you have learned.

Personal
Project

Daydream Believer

By now you will have seen the differences you can make to your life by becoming an assertive person. Have you started asserting yourself yet?

You may be waiting until you reach the end of this book, but is anything else preventing you? Are you waiting until

You get promoted . . .
You've gone on vacation . . .
You get divorced . . .
The children leave home . . .
The next general election . . .
You get a new job . . .
You retire . . .
Someone offers to help. . .
It stops raining . . .
Someone gives you permission . . .

We think you should stop waiting and start the positive process right now!

Final
Thoughts

In closing, we would like to say that the process of becoming a more assertive person does not have to be you versus another person or you versus the rest of the world. With time and practice you will learn to strike a balance between your feelings and those of others, your needs and those of others, your priorities and those of others. When you are able to handle this balance confidently for yourself, your example and your confidence will help others to behave assertively as well. You will be better able to accept responsibility as you make your own choices and build your self-esteem. Here is a final activity to help you on your way.

The Final Step

What would you like to accomplish in the next 12 months? Look again at your Daydream Believer and use it to help you. Do you want to build your own boat in your spare time? Would you like to have a child and become a fulltime homemaker? Do you want to be sitting in the director's chair a year from now?

Write your five goals here.

1. _____

_____

2. _____

_____

3. _____

_____

4. _____

_____

5. _____

_____

How can you work assertively toward achieving your goals?

1. _____

_____

2. _____

_____

3. _____

_____

4. _____

_____

5. _____

_____

Keep this book handy and reread sections as necessary; review the exercises and your thoughts and feelings for as long as you need to. A positive process has been underway since you started reading this book. We hope you are ready to be assertive in your life, and we wish you luck.

About the
Authors

Dr. Barrie Hopson

Barrie is joint chairman of Lifeskills Learning Ltd. Previously he founded the Counseling and Career Development Unit at Leeds University and was the first director until 1984. He has worked widely as a consultant to industrial and educational organizations in the United Kingdom, the United States of America, and Europe. He was responsible for setting up the first career counseling service in British industry in 1970 (at Imperial Chemical Industry) and has since helped a number of organizations in different countries to set up career counseling and career management systems. He is a professional associate of the National Training Laboratories for Applied Behavioral Science in Washington, D.C., a fellow of the British Psychological Society, and of the British Institute of Management.

He has written twenty-two books and numerous articles on personal and career development, marriage, lifeskills teaching, quality service, transition, and change management and generic training skills.

Mike Scally

Mike is joint chairman of Lifeskills Learning Ltd. He combines management training with writing and lecturing. He was Deputy Director of the Counseling and Career Development Unit at Leeds University in 1976 and was involved with its training programs and national projects until 1984.

He has extensive training experience with many of the United Kingdom's major companies and an international reputation in the field of education. He serves on the management committees of and is consultant to many national groups— promoting development education and training at home and abroad.

Mike Scally has written twelve books and many articles on career management, customer service, and lifeskills teaching.